Grace Through the Seasons

Joyce Heiple

ISBN 978-1-63630-039-9 (Paperback)
ISBN 978-1-63630-040-5 (Digital)

Covenant Books, Inc.
11661 Hwy 707
Murrells Inlet, SC 29576
www.covenantbooks.com

To Joz, Kolbe, Lillian, Samuel, Olivia, Luke, Abiti, Joseph, Joey, Abe, and Jameson with the sincere hope that they will always let the grace of God lead them through every season of life.

A special thank you to Terry Wyffels who drew the beautiful cover picture on this book for one of my workshops. She has blessed me with her artistic talent many, many times and has certainly been God's grace for me.

CONTENTS

INTRODUCTION

Some years ago the Lord challenged me to write and give workshops. In spite of my introvert personality, I accepted the challenge and depended upon the Holy Spirit to give me what I needed in words and in courage. I have read many times that the Lord does not call the qualified, but He qualifies the called. He continues to work on that with and in me. After teaching workshops, I finally was inspired to write a book about the defining moments in my life that led to my speaking about *grace*. It shocked me to discover how many people had no idea what *grace* really meant in their lives. Some did not understand the word at all.

Then the Lord encouraged me to share my life in grace so that others could reflect on theirs. I could not help but recall the song "You've Got a Friend in Me" by James Taylor. The lyrics: *Winter, spring, summer, or fall, all you have to do is call and I'll be there, you've got a friend...* spoke strongly to my heart. The life the Lord has given me is full of joys and sorrows, ups and downs. God has been with me every step of the way. The Holy Spirit has convicted me to share this journey with others.

I hope and pray this little book awakens the grace in your soul in order that you may grow closer to our God. I pray that you will either begin or continue to act on the grace that God gives you each and every day. May *grace* be with you!

CHAPTER 1

Grace Defined

Simply defined, *grace* is God's presence in our lives. For many of us, we received *sanctifying grace* at our baptism. Sanctifying grace frees us from the original sin we inherited from Adam and Eve. It also puts within us a yearning for more of the Lord in our lives. That grace never leaves us, but we sometimes turn from it. We have to act on this gift of grace that God so lovingly gave us. It is pure gift, but we need to unwrap it. We can't buy it. We don't earn it. We just receive it because of the love of Almighty God. As you will hear throughout this book, we receive two other types of grace from God: sacramental and actual. These are helps from God to keep the presence of Jesus and the Holy Spirit alive and well in our lives. Without *grace* (God's presence in us), we will not live good lives. We will not make good choices. We will not reach our eternal destiny.

So I ask you to find a comfortable place, grab a pencil, and open your heart as you read the story of my grace life. I share it to inspire you to reflect on yours, to act on yours. Grace is indeed a gift that never leaves us, but we must act on it. We must strive daily to grow closer to Almighty God through His Son Jesus.

The Holy Spirit will point the way. The Holy Spirit will enlighten your heart and heal your wounds as you journey along with me and reflect on your life in *grace*.

CHAPTER 2

Baby Grace

Since we know that *grace* is God's presence in our lives, I think we would all agree that God would have been present at my birth. On June 15, 1949, I was born in Keokuk, Iowa. I guess one could say my birth was a grace-filled moment for my parents. I was the third child born into a family, which would later have a total of eight children. At about two months of age, a big dose of God's grace was poured into my heart when I was baptized into the Catholic Church. This gift, called sanctifying grace, opened the door for me to live a life of grace. The seed was planted, but little Joyce had to someday realize the immensity of the gift, the power of the gift, the responsibility of the gift, and what on earth the gift was going to mean in her life. Baptism was the beginning of my relationship with God. Throughout this book, you will see how grace has influenced my life and my actions. Sanctifying grace did indeed begin my life in grace. I thank my parents for having me baptized. I thank them for giving me the opportunity to live my life in God's loving care.

When were you baptized? Do you grasp the importance of accepting the grace given to you and living your life to use it? God gives the gift, but we have to accept it and use it. Reflect upon how you have lived your life in grace as your continue reading this book. Do you have any thoughts at this very moment about grace as a whole or about your baptism?

_____

_____

_____

_____

_____

_____

_____

_____

_____

_____

_____

_____

_____

_____

_____

_____

_____

_____

_____

_____

JOYCE HEIPLE

One doesn't have a lot of memories in the early years although pictures can help to bring back memories and feelings. We moved from Iowa to Illinois before I turned one year old, so there are certainly no grace-filled memories to share from Iowa except when we went back later to visit my mammo and pop. I think most people would have referred to them as Grandma and Grandpa, but on with the story.

When I was three, I remember—well, kind of remember—climbing out a window on the second floor of our home and having the window shut behind me. There wasn't a screen on the window, and no one else was home except my dad who was sleeping. Someone, I have no idea who, called the fire department.

The firemen rescued me, and my dad got in trouble for not watching me. Do you think God had a hand in taking care of me? I do. He was indeed a present grace in my young life. Our roof wasn't exactly the safest place for a three-year-old child to be climbing around. I would not have survived the fall, so the grace of God wrapped His loving arms around me through a concerned neighbor.

When I was four or five years old, I remember having a really bad earache. What does that have to do with grace, you might already be thinking? Well, my mother's holding me on her lap and praying that my pain would go away is a memory imprinted on my heart. It is probably the only memory I have of my mother's being tender with me, and it was my first experience with prayer.

Was God's presence felt? You better believe it. It is still felt today when I relive the feeling of being held and prayed for by my mother. At that young age, somehow the importance of prayer in times of pain was stored in my memory bank, never to be forgotten.

What about you? How early are your memories of prayer? Did someone model prayer for you? Do you feel God's grace, His presence, when you pray? Do you model prayer for others? Do you have favorite prayers? Do you just talk to God?

_____

_____

_____

_____

_____

_____

_____

_____

_____

_____

_____

_____

_____

_____

_____

_____

_____

_____

_____

_____

_____

_____

_____

_____

_____

_____

_____

_____

_____

JOYCE HEIPLE

_____
_____
_____
_____
_____
_____
_____
_____
_____
_____
_____
_____
_____
_____
_____
_____
_____
_____
_____
_____
_____
_____
_____
_____
_____
_____
_____
_____

We moved down the hill and up the road when I was six. I even remember moving day. It was especially fun because my dad stopped at the tavern at the bottom of the hill and we kids had lots of soda while he drank at the bar. He spent a lot of time drinking at bars.

Later we would experience a lot of pain and emptiness from his life's choices, but at this point in time, it was just fun. After all, Mom was home putting stuff away, so why would we want to be there? She was not very happy upon our return. She wasn't very happy a lot of times when my dad returned from bars. This event is really just a peek into my dad's alcoholic life. The grace for me in this situation is that I learned much from his poor choices, which were many.

My Dado (as we called him) knew God in his heart somewhere, but he pretty much spent the years that I knew him in a self-centered lifestyle, only taking care of his own needs. He missed a lot of special occasions for us kids because of his choices. One of these special occasions in my life was my first communion.

I don't think I had ever felt quite that special in all of my long seven years of living. I looked beautiful in my white dress and white veil that Mom had made for me. I knew I was going to receive Jesus in my heart. I knew I was going to be different and feel different. I knew something was going to change inside of me. Yes, I knew that as a seven-year-old. In the Eucharist I received sacramental grace. The sisters had taught us well.

But Dado wasn't there, and I knew that too. He wasn't there for a lot of our special church happenings or events. The family was growing, so Mom had more responsibilities. As a young child, even if you do not understand the family dynamics, you may still feel the loneliness of a missing parent. I did. Funny thing though, even though my dad chose other things over us kids, we loved him, and we always enjoyed being around him.

A grace in my life concerning my dad occurred during junior high when he played Santa Claus at a big shopping center. We were so proud of him. Our family needed the money, so he took the job. We saw him as a hero to all of those little kids. Sitting at the dining room table together, we would fill envelopes and lick stamps to reply to hundreds and hundreds of letters children had written to Santa Claus—our Dado! God's presence was alive around that table in our joy. *Grace*, you might say? Whenever God grants a beautiful, joyous memory of an otherwise very dysfunctional family, you need to consider it grace.

What about the dysfunctions in your family? Most families have some dysfunctions. Can you find God's grace among the concerns? Can you see Him at work in those who cause you pain? Can you find grace in the pain or after the pain? Ask God now, if needed, for His healing touch. Reflect on the early years in your life. Look for times when you knew God's presence made such a difference. Thank Him for being there for you. Thank Him for helping in your family life.

_____

_____

_____

_____

_____

_____

_____

_____

_____

_____

_____

_____

_____

_____

_____

_____

_____

_____

_____

_____

JOYCE HEIPLE

When I was twelve, our pastor asked me if I would be interested in taking organ lessons and playing for our church. I had only had maybe a year of piano, so this seemed a bit of a challenge, but I eagerly said yes. This was just the beginning of a life-long grace in my journey. Once I started lessons, I found myself spending hours upon hours in church all by myself, practicing on that big pipe organ in the back corner of the church. I would sing up a storm and echo all over the place. I think I actually thought I sounded pretty good. That organ had so many stops on it that I didn't have a clue what they were supposed to do, but I played around with them until I found something that sounded okay.

When I was finished playing, I would walk up to the front of church and sit in front of the statues of Mary and Joseph, talking to them like they were real, as if they were my father and mother. I never really talked much to my mom since she was too busy, and Dad was just not home much. Those visits with Mary and Joseph gave me such peace and inner strength.

The music in my life was indeed a gift, a grace that would bring me back to Jesus over and over again. As the time was drawing closer when I was to sing and play my first 6:30 a.m. mass, a tragedy struck our family. My mom had delivered her eighth child and was having serious headaches, for which the doctor prescribed bed rest. Because she couldn't get that at home with eight children, she went back to Keokuk to stay with her mom and dad for a few days—or at least that was the plan.

The neighbor across the street took my new-born sister to care for while Mom was gone. Our neighbor already had seven children of her own to care for, but she provided grace for our family as she graciously took care of our Laurie.

We got a phone call very late at night, and believe it or not, my dad was actually home. My mom had suffered a very serious stroke at age thirty-four and was barely hanging on to life at my grandparents' house.

My uncle was a chiropractor, and he had found my mother just outside his office, slumped over the steering wheel. After performing a procedure on her that we were later told had probably saved her life, he took her home. My dad had been drinking after work (surprise, surprise), so he was sleeping in his chair when the call came. He needed one of us to go with him to help him stay awake, so I volunteered. Little did I know that I had volunteered for the scariest drive of my life.

We had an old Ford wagon, and I was sitting very close to Dado and jabbering on and on. Jabbering was something I was very good at. I was watching the speed as he got really close to 100 mph. I didn't know a car could go so fast. There weren't many cars on the road, which was a blessing because we were flying.

At 2:00 a.m., we were about halfway there when the car decided to stop in a little town that looked like it was deserted since people are naturally sleeping at that time of night. The gas stations were closed. I thought my dad was going to have a breakdown.

Amazingly, my dad saw a light from a garage down the road. He ran to it and found a man working on his vehicle. The man followed my dad back to our car, and I heard him say he could take a look at it in the morning. My dad said some words I didn't hear well enough to understand, and then the man began working under the hood. Hallelujah, the car started. He warned my dad not to stop or let the engine idle for too long because it might stall out again. I guess he was saying that the fix was temporary.

My dad had tears in his eyes when he got back in the car. He didn't even have any money to give the man. That man was grace from above. That man went beyond what most people would do…just like our God does for us all the time.

Think about your life. Who has been sent by God to get you through hard times or help you encounter miracles on life's journey? Who went the extra mile for you? Did you know and appreciate their actions as being God's actual grace in your life? Do you thank God for the angels He sends to you? Reflect…think…and then thank the Almighty for His ever-present grace in your life.

GRACE THROUGH THE SEASONS

We arrived at my grandma's when the sun was just beginning to come up. Dado and I walked in quietly, but I was certainly not prepared for what I was about to see: my mom looked like she was dead. She looked lifeless. She could not speak, or at least she could not be understood. She was paralyzed.

My uncle recommended renting a vehicle to transport her to Peoria because the hospital in Keokuk was not equipped to help her. I remember so vividly hearing my grandparents say we needed to hurry because Mom was in really bad shape.

Where was God's grace in this moment? As a twelve-year-old girl, I couldn't feel God's grace or see it or even imagine He could help. No one said much to me during these tense moments. It was like I wasn't even there—kind of like I had lived most of my life I guess. I was really scared. Was I going to lose my mom?

I remember talking in the yard out loud to God and to Mary, my heavenly Mother, the same Mary I had talked to so many, many times in church. "Help my mom, Mary. Keep her alive for all of us." I felt grace in the form of calm when I prayed. It seemed like forever, but we transported my mom safely to the hospital. My dad went to see her every day and returned home to tell us about her tiny steps of progress. I remember the excitement we all felt the day she swallowed Jell-O for the first time. The doctor said her recovery was going to be a very long journey, and she might not walk or talk again.

Was the doctor crazy? She had eight children to raise, and my dad wasn't going to do it. The battle seemed long, but she did finally recover, and to the human eye it was a total recovery—a miracle for our family. God's grace was manifested over and over, shining brightly on all of us. God knew we needed our mom, and He knew the longings of our hearts.

What about the miracles in your life? Maybe they aren't life-saving ones and don't seem important to you, but God performs miracles all the time. We just have to learn to notice them and give Him the credit. Where have you experienced divine intervention or God's beautiful gift of grace? Ponder over the beginnings of your life in grace and look for God's presence, His gentle touch, and His gifts. Be quiet and listen to what God has to say to you. Let Him remind you of the miracles you have forgotten.

GRACE THROUGH THE SEASONS

While my mom was in the hospital, I was supposed to play the organ and sing for my first mass. My grandmother had come to stay with us, so she came to the mass with me. Some of you may remember that the Catholic Church used to have masses in Latin. This was back in 1963. Did anyone ever teach me the Latin? No! I just made the words up as I sang; no one knew what I was singing anyway. It's rather funny when I look back, but I was singing up a storm.

I was really falling in love with playing and singing in my church, even if it was at six thirty in the morning and I am not a morning person. I had to walk a long way to get to church, so I had quite the reputation of walking in about five minutes late. The truth is, I was really happy when my 6:30 a.m. duties were all over.

My services were a source of cheap labor, so I was not fired for being late. Actually, back in those days I received $1 for every mass I played. Sometimes I got a check for $30 or $40 a month. I was rich and richly blessed at the same time. Music had become for me a way to feel God's grace in my life. He was present with me as I played and sang His praises or when I played for funerals.

The people in the parish loved their new young musician. I really wasn't very good, but no one ever told me so. The self-esteem I so lacked in my home life was abundant in my music. I began playing in church when I was thirteen, and today in my seventies, I still play in spite of the fact that I had no formal training. I still make lots of mistakes, but God has blessed me over and over and over through music. He gave me the gift. I give it back to Him.

What gifts have you been given that you have not used for God's glory? What gifts have you been given that you could use to share God's grace with others? Have you experienced His grace by using your gifts? Do you acknowledge your gifts as grace? Before you go on to the next chapter, take time and reflect on your childhood with God, your heavenly Father. Listen and pray as you reflect.

_____

_____

_____

_____

_____

_____

_____

_____

_____

_____

_____

_____

_____

_____

_____

_____

_____

_____

_____

_____

_____

GRACE THROUGH THE SEASONS

_____
_____
_____
_____
_____
_____
_____
_____
_____
_____
_____
_____
_____
_____
_____
_____
_____
_____
_____
_____
_____
_____
_____
_____
_____
_____
_____
_____
_____

CHAPTER 3

Those Grace-Filled Teenage Years

Someone has said that we forget the junior high years because they are such painful ones. I think that statement may be right. I don't have many pleasant memories during those years except for my music in church. We had small classes at St. Cecilia's Catholic School where I attended, but I was not one of the popular kids. For example, I didn't make the cheerleading squad.

Life at home was pretty much "survival of the fittest," I always said. Mom was so busy taking care of the eight of us, and Dad was not home much, so we kids just did our own things.

I received the sacrament of Confirmation in eighth grade. I don't think I had a clue what I was receiving at the time. I just knew I had to memorize a big part of the catechism in case the bishop asked me a question. He didn't. Thank God! Our class didn't even get to pick our own sponsors. A sponsor is a person chosen to be an example for you in your faith life. *What a rip-off!* I do know that at my confirmation, I was supposed to have received some type of grace from the Holy Spirit that would allow Him to be more active in my life. If that were the case, why was I always so lonely? Why did I have only a few friends? What was missing in my life? Where were all these gifts I was supposed to receive?

In eighth grade my teacher and I formed a bond that even today, fifty-plus years later, we still communicate, at least at Christmas. She became my lifeline throughout high school. I always knew I could go talk with Sister Margaret Alice. She had time for me. She seemed to know I had a hole in my heart. When she was around, I knew someone cared.

I met Rob when I was a freshman in high school. It didn't take me too long to figure out that it felt good to have someone else who cared for me. We dated on and off through high school, and we were indeed falling in love.

Rob and I would go to see Sister Margaret Alice together every once in a while. That was really grace at work. She listened to both of us on these visits.

God put her in my life for comfort, for wisdom, for direction, and for love. I was crushed when her order moved her away, but by then I was a little more stable. I guess God knew it was time for me to grow up a little.

During my high school years, my mother would sometimes make me break up with Rob for fear of me making poor choices. Rob seemed to enjoy the breakups and would date other girls during our time apart. I just waited and felt the poignant loneliness until we got back together.

In the spring of our senior year, Rob told me he had decided to go to the seminary. Wow! That was a shocker. So we broke up again. We thought it best to attempt to stay apart since he was going to turn his life over to God—or so he thought.

During this time frame, I discovered that my father was having an affair. Little did I know that he had had many affairs throughout his marriage, and this woman was the one he always seemed to go back to. In my youthful stupidity, I decided I was going to follow him, catch him, and confront the two of them. I still don't know if God approved of this idea, but I do know He was with me every step of the way.

Talk about a soap opera story. I did just as I had planned: I followed and I waited. When I finally knocked on her door, she answered in a nightgown of sorts. I pushed my way into her house while she screamed at me, calling me a very unkind name. She grabbed my brand-new white furry coat and tore it. I was so proud of that coat since I had purchased it myself. I'll never forget that coat, but I was never able to wear it again.

My dad walked out of her bedroom in his underwear, obviously hungover. He told me to go home, that we would talk later. Talk—that was a joke! My dad and I never talked.

I remember a few days later his coming to my room and telling me he was sorry I had gone there. He said there were things I just didn't understand. That was it. He turned and left the room. The relationship with this other woman continued, but I said nothing more. I felt so alone. I went to see Rob after I left her house because I needed to feel loved by someone. He appreciated my attention, but he really didn't have what I needed. He couldn't make my loneliness or emptiness go away.

What I needed was a relationship with God, but I didn't seem to know that. I played music every Sunday until I was eighteen, but that was all—I just went to church. I didn't really know my God. I didn't have a relationship with Him. I went to Catholic school for twelve years, so I had certainly learned lots of facts. I had even attended a retreat or two and certainly grown closer to God, but I still did not have a relationship.

Have you ever felt like you were just going through the motions at church and not really working on developing a relationship with God? Were your teenage years tough ones? Do you have memories where God was a part of your teenage life? Did you experience loneliness in your family or with friends? What was your relationship with God like during those years? Talk to God about it. Listen...

_____
_____
_____
_____
_____
_____
_____
_____
_____
_____
_____
_____
_____
_____
_____
_____
_____
_____
_____
_____
_____

GRACE THROUGH THE SEASONS

I wish I had known then that loneliness was a time to work on godliness and that loneliness can actually be a grace to cause you to grow closer to God. I didn't have a clue about making good use of this time; I only ached inside and didn't even know why.

Rob and I both left for college in the fall. He went to the seminary, and I went to Quincy College with dreams of becoming a social worker. I thought that maybe someday I could help people in crazy, messed-up families.

I was so lonely at college. I wasn't very good at making friends, it seemed. My best friend from high school was at the same college, but we never saw each other. During that first year of college, Rob came to see me once, and I went to where he was studying once. We just couldn't seem to make a clean break.

I discovered there was a noon mass each day at school and began attending. Oh, what a grace! I began talking to God and telling Him how I was feeling: *I just want to feel loved.*

Well, love was just around the corner it seemed. Rob decided to quit school at the end of the semester. His grades were low, and he was doubting a real call to the priesthood. I decided to quit too. I decided the junior college at home was just fine and so much cheaper. I missed being at home and was worried about my parents.

Or was it that I really just wanted to be where Rob was? It didn't take too long for me to realize this was the case, and we were engaged. I was still a teenager. I was still a baby Catholic in my mind. I had so much to learn about my faith, myself, and my loneliness. Marriage was going to be the answer for me. I would feel loved. Someone would finally be there for me. On May 3, 1969, about six weeks before I turned twenty, Rob and I were married.

Hey, good news! My dad did walk me down the aisle, and he even teared up a little. Rob came to the wedding whiter than a sheet after a great deal of drinking the night before. His drinking should have set off an alarm, but a girl oftentimes marries someone a lot like her father.

Okay, it's your turn to go down memory lane through your teenage years. I hope it isn't too painful. I pray you can see the love of God on your journey. God was with me when I confronted the unfaithfulness of my dad. He was definitely with me when I was at college. He wiped every tear of loneliness I shed.

He was with us on a beautiful wedding day. My dad helped make it special, but my heavenly Father blessed it and graced us with the sacrament of marriage. Through that sacrament we received sacramental grace that would certainly come in handy in the years to come. Where did you sense His presence in the early years of your marriage?

Where do you wish you had reached out to Him but didn't? What would you like to say to God now about those teenage years? Do you need healing in your life from those years? Ask for God's healing grace. Ask for the painful memories to be released.

CHAPTER 4

Grace in Early Married Life

The Vietnam War was going on, and Rob had enlisted in the Naval Reserve so he wouldn't get drafted. After our beautiful wedding mass in May, he left on an airplane for California in September. I was super blessed with the opportunity to drive out there at the end of October and join him in military housing.

My mom drove out with me, and we had a memorable time. I had never had Mom all to myself before, so it was indeed a grace from above. We laughed and laughed at so many things along the way.

Life was good! Rob and I were together again—at least until he left for 199 days at sea. While he was gone, I was of course lonely again, and he was not the only thing missing from my life. Music was gone. Mass was gone. Jesus seemed to be absent. I was just existing until I found a local church where I would go to occasional masses and cry and talk to my God. Oh my, those were grace-filled moments!

I got a job in San Pedro, California, at the Harbor Area Retarded Children's Center. That was what it was called in 1970. I had my own class of eight wonderful children. This group was truly a gift from the Lord.

This position seemed to fall in my lap, and my faith told me how I really found the job. God was gracing me even when I was not being so good to Him. God never left my side. I couldn't stop telling God how thankful I was. My gratitude prompted me to go to church a little more. When Rob returned from his travels, something seemed different, but I didn't have a clue what it was.

We spent another year in California in the Navy and then came home to Illinois to begin our family. Robbie III's birth was indeed *amazing grace!* We went to a nearby church to have him baptized, and in their bulletin was a plea for an organist. God was calling, and I answered. We went to church every time I played. It wasn't a big commitment, but music was working its magic in my life once again. Jason was born two years later, another precious gift from God.

We were still attending the same church, so we had him baptized there.

I had stopped playing the organ because it just wasn't like when I was young. It seemed my playing wasn't good enough, or at least that was my perception. I began to feel like I wasn't good enough for God either. Since our firstborn was getting close to school age, we began looking to move out of the city. We found an old, old farmhouse just down the road from a beautiful country church called St. Mary of Lourdes. It was time for our Robbie to go to religious instruction, so we started going to church again.

You will never guess what was in the bulletin. Yes, you are correct. They were looking for an organist. Jesus was opening my heart once again through His gift of music. I started playing and started going to church almost every week.

Child number three, Jessica, was born while we still lived in our farmhouse, and life seemed to be fairly normal. She was a beautiful gift from God.

We moved from the farmhouse into a home where I could run a licensed preschool in our lower level. I was quite busy being a mom, a preschool teacher, a homemaker, a college student, and a wife. I believe I was a Cub Scout den mother during this time too, but that was a short-lived commitment. While I was busy, busy, busy, Rob was working and stopping after work to do more drinking (much like my dad used to do). Although he was quite self-centered (again, kind of like my dad), I really didn't notice his behavior too much because it was what I was used to.

I thought our marriage was doing fine. We didn't fight, we seemed to get along, and I thought I was a good wife. However, I still felt that pang of loneliness though I sure didn't understand where it came from and why I felt so empty so often. I seemed to be going through the motions of existing. I didn't have a close relationship with my husband or my God. It is no wonder I felt lonely since I was missing what was most important in my life. I didn't have a clue.

Grace is always present within us and around us. Knowing that, we need to claim the grace. Many of us go through life lonely, not accepting the gift within. God is yearning for us to develop a love relationship with Him. Are you experiencing loneliness now, or have you at other times in your married years? Do you call on the grace available in the sacrament of marriage to replenish or strengthen your relationship? God needs to be the center of your marriage. But even before that, He needs to be the center of your life. Is He? Talk to Him about where He is in your life. Talk to Him about where He was in your life in your beginning years of marriage. Thank Him for the blessings. Thank Him for His presence. Thank Him for His healing.

GRACE THROUGH THE SEASONS

_____

_____

_____

_____

_____

_____

_____

_____

_____

_____

_____

_____

_____

_____

_____

_____

_____

_____

_____

_____

_____

_____

_____

_____

_____

_____

_____

_____

_____

CHAPTER 5

Grace through My Cross

The day of my sister Laurie's wedding and my sister Kathy's twenty-first birthday was full of family celebration. My dad was even there although things weren't going too well between my mom and dad at the time. It was indeed a day I will never forget.

After the wedding we went to a tavern to celebrate with my sister—or at least Rob was celebrating. He had been doing a lot of drinking throughout the day, and I remember being worried that he was the one driving us home. When we got home, he told me to sit down because he had something to say. I certainly thought his words sounded strange. He wasn't usually much of a talker, and neither was I for that matter. He seemed nervous, and I didn't have a clue what was going on. He didn't sit next to me. He sat across from me in the green chair. I remember it like it was yesterday.

I believe I started the conversation by saying something like, "What's up?"

Very quickly the following sentence poured out of his mouth: "I want a divorce, I am having an affair, and I am in love with her."

To this day, even forty years later, that sentence still takes my breath away. I didn't have a clue. I only knew he had been gone more and drinking more…just like my dad had done. I didn't know he was attached to another woman…just like my dad was. Rob had met her through work, and they drank together after work. The story goes on from there like another soap opera.

But here I was, seated in my home around midnight, looking at the man I thought loved me— the father of our three children, the provider of our home, the man who said he would love me forever. If I had ever felt alone before, I really felt alone now.

Where in the world was this God who supposedly loved me? Why would He let this happen to our happy family? What happy family—who was I kidding? I took the car keys and left for a friend's house.

On the way there, I actually contemplated running off the road but resolved very quickly not to do that to my kids. My friend listened to me for hours and basically told me to get rid of the bum. I returned home in time to shower, change, and go to Sunday mass.

I wasn't scheduled to play the organ that day, and I didn't want my church community to see my red and swollen eyes, so I drove to another town close by. I sat almost in the back and cried most of the way through the service. I remember vividly staring up at the huge crucifix and pleading with Jesus to save my marriage. My heart and soul were touched with this clear message from above: *"Joyce, I love you. Keep loving Rob, and I will bless your family."* To me it seemed to be God's way of saying, "Hang in there, girl, and Rob will get his act together." Those words were an outpouring of His love!

God's grace was touching my humanness and giving me the courage I would need so badly in the days, weeks, and months ahead. I left church and went to my parents' house. As my mom and dad sat at the kitchen table, I told them about the affair. My dad, who had experienced numerous extra-marital relationships, told me to forgive him once but never let him do it to me again. I have often wondered what my mom was thinking when he said that. I have also wondered if she really loved my dad or if it was her faith that kept them together. She must have really grabbed on to the grace in her life. So I decided to try to grab onto that grace too.

Monday morning I had to go to college and take two final exams. I share this information because without a doubt God aced those tests for me. I hadn't been to sleep yet and hadn't opened a textbook to study. God knew I needed His help because I was physically and emotionally about to collapse.

Ironically, one of the classes I was taking was called "Marriage and the Family." When I went back the next day to ask for my grade and the professor told me I had a perfect score, I fell apart. He was such a nice man, and he didn't have a clue as to why one of his students would start bawling after such good news. He was staring at me as I responded, "I aced the class but failed the course." I think he figured out what must have been going on when I ran off.

The other "A" on a final exam was in my political science course. I hadn't even opened the text, I didn't like the subject, and I really wanted to drop the class but hadn't bothered to do so. I was counting on a solid "C" on the final. When I learned that I had gotten an "A," I decided God must like political science and He must have read those chapters. How else could I have gotten an "A"? What a grace that was in my life! Failure in college would not have been a good mix with the failure I was already feeling in my life.

I was trying to keep things normal at home, but how normal can life be when you are living with a man who says he loves someone else? I was walking on eggshells all of the time, trying to be the perfect wife. Basically I was just surviving. Because it was almost Christmas, I think we were pretending for the three kids. In fact, I don't think it; I know it. Shortly after Christmas, Rob announced that he was leaving to live with his mother. He couldn't live with the other woman because she also happened to be married. The whole situation was so crazy! What was he thinking? I know, he wasn't thinking!

Rob packed his clothes in paper sacks and then sat on the living room floor to tell our eight-year-old and our six-year-old that he was leaving because he loved someone else. If I hadn't been sick before, listening to him speak those words to the children made me ill. How could he?

God, you can come into this situation anytime now. I'm waiting for You. I'm waiting for the grace to understand. I'm waiting for a miracle. I'm waiting for this pain to go away. I'm waiting for answers, Lord! Where are You?

The answers did not come, but God's grace did. Not becoming angry at Rob required a special grace, and it became harder and harder for me to pray. I was so empty, so lonely, so devastated. Sometimes I would send the three kids out to play so that I could go up to my room and literally scream at God.

Rob's uncle Frank was my lifeline. I would call him often, and he would pray for me over the phone. At times he would come over and sit with me and the kids, just being present and encouraging me to keep loving Rob. He would say, "Joyce, love will win in the end." Love did win in the end. God did keep His promise, and He did bless our family. God's grace allowed me to forgive Rob and to grow more in love with him.

Uncle Frank's example encouraged me through the tough times, and God's grace carried me. I began praying more often and more than just desperation prayers. I joined a prayer group with some friends from church. This charismatic group really gave me the strength I needed. Although I had received the Holy Spirit at my confirmation, I sensed the Spirit coming alive in my life. I actually could feel Him working. "Amen, amen, I say to you, unless a grain of wheat falls to the ground and dies, it remains just a grain of wheat; but if it dies, it produces much fruit" (John 12:24). Yes, indeed I had died with Christ. I had finally realized that peace was replacing my devastation, my total emptiness, my crumbled marriage.

When Rob left, I had decisions to make. I chose to continue loving him, treating him like I loved him, and believing that God would win over his hardened heart. I chose to ignore all the friends around me who were saying he wasn't coming home and I should let him have the divorce. I chose to believe God would bless our family. I chose to rise above the pain and live through it. God was gracing me abundantly. Was it easy? *No*! Was it what God wanted for our family? *Yes*, indeed it was!

All of us encounter hard times in our lives. How we respond to them makes or breaks us. Do we use the grace God has for us? Do we allow God to intervene at His pace and in His time?

Reflect on your painful moments, on the times when you wondered where God was. Can you see the grace now? Can you see what God taught you through your pain? Can you thank God at this point in your life for that pain? Where did you sense His presence? Do you still have someone to forgive who caused you pain? There is no time like the present to ask for a forgiving heart…healing is a grace from God. Ask for it. Accept it. If you are still in the midst of a painful situation, keep moving…there is light at the end of the tunnel. Don't get stuck.

GRACE THROUGH THE SEASONS

CHAPTER 6

Grace Walking through the Pain

Rob had been gone for six weeks. It seemed more like six years. My prayer life had certainly changed during that time as I discovered how badly I needed to trust my God. I talked to Him every day about how I was going to get through the day. I was still in college and now ever so convicted to finish. I knew I needed more security for the kids' and my future. I had someone else teaching my preschool so I could devote more time to finishing my degree. God was my constant companion during my studying, and I'll always give Him credit for the good grades I received.

The night Rob came home, he had obviously been drinking a lot. He actually had been to the house earlier in the day to see the children. I had given him a long, long letter and asked him to really read it. The letter was the pouring out of my heart and soul to him for our marriage and our family. I prayed and cried the entire time I wrote that letter. I knew it was of God, so I left the results up to Him. God's grace was abundant when I wrote it, and I knew it would be there also when Rob read it.

Rob sat down at the kitchen table and said, "I am home to stay." At that time, he also admitted to me that he had had relations with someone when he was overseas. I had sensed something was different when he returned home but wouldn't have given unfaithfulness a second thought as the possible reason. Then he rattled on a lot about his drinking and his selfishness. I knew it was the alcohol talking, but my heart was so relieved that he was sitting there. He was *home*. He continued to talk, and I continued to thank God for bringing him home.

He said he didn't want me to talk about the other woman anymore. The whole situation was to be forgotten. I did not argue; I was just so glad Rob was home. My mom had never brought up my dad's issues with him either. I guess someone forgot to tell the other woman that Rob had chosen to come home because she wasn't giving up easily. She even called me and told me he wouldn't stay with me, so I should let him go. After I talked to her briefly about God, she hung up.

I must admit that Rob's presence at home did not mean things were fine. They were actually far from fine. My sense of self-worth had taken a nose-dive, and I had no idea if he loved me or if he still loved the other woman. I couldn't bring myself to talk about it. I just went on living and talked to God about my emptiness. Our marriage struggled, and Rob personally struggled over the next few years. He finally made a clean break with the other woman, but not with alcohol. I decided I couldn't change him. However, I needed to focus on my life and my relationship with God if I was going to be a survivor. I went to a counselor for a while, but what helped me the most was when I was asked to do the music (there's that music again) for our charismatic prayer group.

I would spend hours each week reading Scripture, listening to songs, and listening to the Spirit as a part of planning the music for the next prayer meeting. I grew more in tune with the gentle whispers from the Holy Spirit in my life. I felt more at peace than ever before. Did I have a happy marriage? *It was better because I was better.* I found something that I had needed all along—a relationship with Almighty God. I was seeking God and not man to fill the hole in my heart. I was falling in love with my God. Praise the Lord for His grace in my life. Meanwhile I believe Rob was noticing something different about me.

Rob told me one day in church that he had pleaded with God to do something in his life because he was truly losing his faith. That same day a close friend of ours came to the house and signed Rob up for the program called Cursillo. This was truly a "God-incident." Rob seemed to sense it was a God-calling. Cursillo is a special weekend retreat that presents the Catholic faith in a very personal way. Some define it as a short course in Christianity. I define it as a miracle weekend in Rob's life.

Cursillo was the beginning of a new walk, a new journey for Rob. He began a transformation that God continues to grace and bless on a daily basis. Rob discovered that he had to forgive himself for hurting his wife and children as he journeyed through his pain.

Cursillo and the love of His gracious God enabled him to do just that. As he grew closer to the Lord, our marriage began finding God at its center. It was like we had turned a corner. Rob was on fire for the Lord, studying the Bible, and helping with the youth group. God's grace was shining from him.

Sometimes we have to walk through the muck in our lives. Sometimes we have to feel it, to live it, to embrace it, and to grow through it. We have to let God teach us to turn our crosses into bridges. Take some time to think about your crosses, the pain you may have experienced in your married life or in other areas of your life. Have you cried out for God's grace? Have you felt it? Have you felt abandoned? Did you keep journeying through the abandonment? Did you get stuck? Can you look back at the journey and see God's presence? What do you and the Lord need to say to each other about this time in your life? Give God plenty of time to minister to you. Listen to Him. Feel His healing touch. Receive His spirit of love and healing.

_____

_____

_____

_____

_____

_____

_____

_____

_____

_____

_____

_____

_____

_____

_____

_____

GRACE THROUGH THE SEASONS

CHAPTER 7

Finding God on the Journey

Rob and I were both very involved in our Christian walk. We were on Cursillo teams, Marriage Encounter teams, Retourno teams, Watch teams, TEC (Teens Encounter Christ) teams, and I even tried a prison team. The Marriage Encounter and Retourno teams were set up to enrich marriages through Scripture and discussion. The Watch team was parish-based to build community and faith. We were immersed in sharing our faith with others. On our first of many, many TEC teams, the Lord began breaking down a wall that remained between us. It had been nine years since Rob's return home, and we really hadn't discussed what happened while he was away.

On the TEC team, we were asked to give the marriage talk. We had built a strong wall between us, so each team event allowed us to remove or loosen a brick or two. We have been on many TEC teams since that first one and have given that talk so many times. Some of the wall is still present in our relationship, but God has been easing the pain as we are growing in our love for God and each other.

After I graduated from college at the age of thirty-three, I got a call from the superintendent at a neighboring school. I didn't know him, but he had heard about my preschool, and he needed a second-grade teacher. After talking for a minute or two, he asked me if I wanted the job. God's grace has come in so many ways in my life. I was excited, but school was to start in only two weeks. I went in the next day to meet the superintendent, and he took me to my classroom. As I looked in all of the other rooms, I could see that they were creatively decorated and ready to go. However, my classroom was empty except for my desk and the children's desks. I sat at my desk, put my head down, and cried. How in the world was I going to do this? Where should I begin?

After a few tears, a calm came over me. I knew God had given me this job, and God wasn't about to leave me now. In a week I was ready. I was bursting with energy and ready to meet my class. Teaching second grade was my niche. It really built my self-worth.

The students loved me, and the parents seemed to think I was okay. This teaching job was indeed a God-given gift.

After about seven years, I felt a calling on the inside, stirring me to write a program to teach values at the school. I was petrified to approach the superintendent about my idea, but he was very receptive. The Lord and I wrote stories, composed songs, and found awesome puppets. The program became known as the Can-Do Program. The students were called the Can-Do kids, and I was the Can-Do teacher. The whole idea came from my love of Philippians 4:13 (ESV), where St. Paul writes, "I can do all things through him who strengthens me." I still taught my own class of second graders, but I was given a release day once per month to teach Can-Do. Oh, the kids loved it!

I was in my tenth year of teaching and still loving every minute of it when my neighbor started talking to me about a program at the local university, which the federal government was funding. She said I could become a licensed school counselor in just three years. For weeks I told her absolutely no. Why would I? I loved teaching. Then one day she said I could make a difference in more lives than just the twenty in my classroom. Her words stuck in my heart, and I began to hear the invitation from within as I argued with God, *It would take too much time. I am too old to go back to school. I already have my second graders. I have three children and a husband at home. Leave me alone, God.*

One morning after taking my students to PE, I decided to call the university just to ask for information. Before I hung up, I had agreed to take the entrance exam that same afternoon. Now I had to walk into my superintendent's office, ask him for the afternoon off, and tell him why. He said, "Joyce, you may certainly go take the exam and take the courses, but we will not be hiring a school counselor when you are finished."

I went to the university and took the test. The test was made up of analogies, and I don't think that way. When I started, I told God that I trusted Him to pass the test for me as He had done ten years before. Then I registered for two classes and bought the books. The Holy Spirit was alive in my heart and in my actions.

By the way, I failed the entrance test. God didn't bail me out this time. Due to my honors GPA at the bachelor's level and several good letters of recommendation, I was allowed to enter the program on probation. *What a way to start, Lord!* To make a long story short, I did very well in the program. The superintendent allowed me to do my internship at our school. During my internship, the parents from our school decided they needed me as their school counselor. The school board meeting was overrun with supporters, so the board voted yes to hire me as the first school counselor.

Do you think God had His hand in this decision? Do you think that from the very beginning God had planned this opportunity for me? I sure do.

The courses were really hard, and it was difficult to find time to study while teaching school, continuing with the Can-Do Program, and being a wife and mom. However, something was different in my school experience this time: I had a supportive husband. Rob helped me find the time to get everything done. My school counseling years were great! God graced me with the gift of compassion. I listened. I learned. I loved.

At Rob's third Cursillo weekend, he was finally convicted to quit drinking alcohol. Throughout the team preparation, he would come home and share that the talks all seemed to include someone's troubles with alcohol. I prayed really hard that he would hear what the Lord was saying to him. One Sunday evening I picked him up, and with tears streaming down his face, he told me he would *never* drink again. Through the absolute *grace* of God, he never has.

Just a few months after that decision, he surrendered to God and agreed to apply for the diaconate. Yes, the man who had left his wife and three children to live a life of regret was now being transformed into a man of service to our God. I have always said I believe in miracles, but all I have to do is look at the man I love to see a walking, talking picture of God's grace in action. The diaconate involved four and one-half years of training. In our diocese, the husband and wife did it together.

I had been praying for so long that we would be involved in some sort of ministry together. This was indeed God answering my prayer. We not only spent that four and one-half years of training together, but we also continued on the staff another ten years to help other candidates go through the program. What God can do in a life that answers His call and follows His lead is truly amazing.

The Cursillo program blessed my life many times over. I was saturated in God's grace when asked to be rectora (leader) fourteen years after my initial weekend. Nonetheless, both of us were so busy on teams and doing God's work that we didn't have time to really work on us, to really heal our marriage.

Has God called on you to do His work? Did you answer His call? If you did, do you find the work just busy work, or does it help you grow closer to Him? Reflect on the work you do, the ministries you are involved in, the groups you assist with. Do they help in your relationship with God, or do they just build your ego? What we want in life is more of You, Lord, and less of ourselves. Send us work that will enable that to happen. Many times I have asked the Lord, "What do want of me, Lord?" Sometimes I am almost fearful of His answer. I didn't want to go to school at age thirty or forty-five, but God's grace carried me and blessed me abundantly in so many ways. Ask Him today that same question. Be still and listen for His answer.

_____
_____
_____
_____
_____
_____
_____
_____
_____
_____
_____
_____
_____
_____
_____

GRACE THROUGH THE SEASONS

_____

_____

_____

_____

_____

_____

_____

_____

_____

_____

_____

_____

_____

_____

_____

_____

_____

_____

_____

_____

_____

_____

_____

_____

_____

_____

_____

_____

_____

CHAPTER 8

Pain's Surprise Return

Just two months after Rob was ordained, I was given the privilege of going on a twelve-day pilgrimage to Italy by myself. Rob did not want to go, so I went alone, all expenses paid. Something inside of me had begun stirring at his ordination. Rob had grown so much in the Lord, and my heart seemed to be asking God what He wanted of me. *Okay, Lord, I am going to a whole list of holy places, so certainly You will reveal to me what it is You want of me now.*

I knelt before the cross of San Damiano—that very cross at which Jesus spoke to St. Francis. I asked.

I listened. That night I cried myself to sleep. The next day I knelt in the chapel called Portiuncula, where Jesus spoke to Francis and St. Francis founded his order. I was there for a long time. I listened. I waited. I listened. Finally I heard, "Joyce, I want you to love more."

I am surprised no one around me noticed my reaction. In shock I said, "I do love, Lord." Well, that was the end of our conversation. That was my big revelation. It was one that would take me many years to really grasp. I received a big amount of grace from God that day, but at the time I didn't get it.

A year after my Italy trip, my school sent me to St. Louis for a school counselors' convention. I took a book with me to read in the evenings because I wasn't the social type who did a lot of networking at these kinds of things. The book I read seemed to awaken something in me. Little did I know that it was the grace of the Holy Spirit intervening in my life. I read the book two times and began writing.

During that weekend, the Lord and I wrote a workshop about the Mary and Martha story. This was the story on which the book I had read was based. Holy Spirit fire was alive in my heart. On my drive home, I distinctly remember asking the Lord who He had in mind to do this workshop.

I had given talks to parents from a school counselor's perspective but never led a spiritual workshop. *Not me, Lord!* I argued. However, God doesn't call the qualified; He qualifies the called. A few months after that, I began doing the Mary and Martha workshop all over the diocese. It was such a grace in my life. I would come away from each workshop on fire with God's love.

I started reading other spiritual books and writing workshops based on what I was learning. I came upon a book called *The Peace Prayer,* written basically about loving more. The words from Assisi came back to me loud and clear. *Yes, Lord, I hear You! I need to love more.* It's been over fifteen years since that conference in St. Louis, and the Lord is still helping me write and give workshops and Lenten reflections. We even wrote one about the Seasons of Grace in our lives. His grace has been abundant to me when I sit down and write for Him. His grace is even more abundant when this introvert stands behind a podium and speaks for Him. Oh, God is so good to me!

After Rob was ordained a deacon, which was indeed a grace-filled day and a miracle in action, he was asked to be the spiritual director of the TEC program. I was so excited for him. I automatically assumed that he would want me to be his assistant. After all, I had helped him every step of the way throughout his diaconate training, and I was very active in the TEC program. Why wouldn't I assist him?

When I asked Rob about my assisting, he responded very quickly, "No, I can't work with you." He may as well have driven a knife into my heart. In my eyes he was rejecting me all over again. I ran off and buried my hurt as I had always done as I had learned from my mom. I cried like I had done when he left me. Approximately twenty-five years after that devastating time, all of the pain I thought I had buried so well came right back to the surface. *Oh, God, why does it hurt so bad?* Why did I feel so alone, so rejected, and so unloved just because he said no? He didn't even know he had upset me, so I just let it go.

A short time after that, I began a class to learn to be a spiritual director, certified to walk with someone on their spiritual journey. This was yet another scary leap God was asking of me because I didn't feel worthy. During the two-year training period, we were asked to do a lot of self-reflection in order to receive spiritual direction ourselves.

On one particular retreat weekend, I spent some time with the teacher of our class in spiritual direction. He pretty much demanded that when I went home, I was to tell my husband that I needed him to go to marriage counseling for my sake. The thought of confronting Rob scared me quite a bit. Even after all of the years, Rob didn't want to go there. He didn't see the need to bring up the past. But I asked him to do it for me.

We went to two sessions. Were we healed? No. Did it help? Well, at least Rob said he was sorry, and I heard him explain why he thought he had done it. When the therapist brought up alcohol, Rob became defensive and wouldn't go back. I must admit that he did go to counseling for me. He did just what I asked. The truth is the pain of rejection was my problem, not really his. God and I had to work on that. I had to believe I was God's child and that His love for me was all that really mattered. Rob's love and acceptance were of course important, but my relationship with God had to take the front seat in my life.

How about you and your pain in life? Has it ever reared its ugly head after you thought it was gone? Have you had to deal with it again and again? Does your pain help you grow closer in your faith walk? If not, what are you doing wrong? Have you forgiven whoever caused the pain—not just once, but over and over again? Have you discovered that pain can be a gift?

Once you are through it, you can gaze upon the grace God gifted you with to survive it. Everyone has encountered some type of pain in their lives. Spend some time looking back and praising God for the growth you have seen in spite of the pain.

_____

_____

_____

_____

_____

_____

_____

_____

_____

_____

_____

_____

_____

_____

_____

_____

_____

GRACE THROUGH THE SEASONS

_____

_____

_____

_____

_____

_____

_____

_____

_____

_____

_____

_____

_____

_____

_____

_____

_____

_____

_____

_____

_____

_____

_____

_____

_____

_____

_____

CHAPTER 9

Prayer through the Seasons

My prayer life has been as varied as the weather in the seasons of life. In my early years I felt a need to pray, a longing to pray, but did not seem to know how except to talk to the statues in church and recite rote prayers.

In times of trouble and pain I learned really quick how to call out to God for help, for healing, for answers. So often during these times I would forget that prayer is a two-way street. I was so busy crying out I would forget the listening part.

I have learned that real prayer is a conversation with God. Whether I am praising Him, petitioning Him, or thanking Him, I need to be still and wait for His response. It may come in a feeling. It may come in the gentle whispers; but it will come.

I have gone through dry seasons of prayer when I was pretty sure God had abandoned me. I felt so empty and alone. Sometimes I would get angry with Him for not responding, not lightening my load. He accepted my anger. He knew what I was going through. Sometimes my prayer life has been like the driest desert with no refreshment, no encouragement, and no apparent response.

But here's the thing. God has never given up on me. He walked with me through the desert, through the abandonment. He kept just enough light shining that I could keep walking through the tunnel of despair.

Some of my favorite prayer happenings are through music. I listen to a song and am sure that God is sitting right next to me, telling me what it means for me. There was a time I was very discouraged with a workshop I was giving at our church because no one had signed up. I was fussing with God, telling Him I was finished. I was doing no more of these crazy workshops. I turned on the radio and "Voice of Truth" by Casting Crowns was on. God said: *Whose voice are you listening to, Joyce?*

Every single day that Rob was gone from home I listened to the song "I Believe in You" by Don Williams. My God kept telling to believe in Him and in Rob. Every night before I went to sleep I would sing the song "I Believe in the Sun" by Carey Landry and the Lord would give me peace and belief that a miracle was going to happen in my life. The song "More of You" by Don Moen became the theme for all of my workshops because that was what I was yearning for in my life. I prayed that every time I spoke, the listeners would yearn for more of the Lord in their lives. Yes indeed, music is probably the number one source of prayer for me. It opens my heart and my soul for communication with Almighty God in a powerful way.

Nature is also a way to connect with my friend Jesus. I sit in our sunroom or out on the deck, close my eyes, and let the birds speak to my soul. Oh, such peace! I particularly love the springtime because the new growth, the awesomeness of flowering trees, the brightness of spring flowers, all lead me to thankfulness and a spirit of joy.

Prayerfulness in solitude is still hard for me after all these years, but I keep trying. My mind is so busy it always wants to talk to God and tell Him so many things.

I like to go on walks. When I do so, I go through my whole family, one person at a time, and talk to God about them and what is going on in their life. This talk usually includes my friends and people on my prayer list too. Once again, I am so busy telling God stuff that on these walks He doesn't get much of a chance to respond; but I know He is listening.

Mass and Communion are top of the list for me and people of my faith. Receiving the sacraments is such a gift, such a blessing from Jesus.

I do love to read the Bible too. I do Lectio Divina at times. It is a special way to read chapters of the Bible and meditate so that the Holy Spirit has time to speak to my heart. It is important to me to talk to God at the beginning of every day and at the end of every day. At the beginning I ask Him to open my eyes to where I might be needed that day or who I might encounter. I intentionally ask for the grace to accomplish whatever He might ask of me. At the end of the day I ask for forgiveness for anything I didn't do that He might have asked of me or if I have wronged my God in any way. Do I forget sometimes? Of course I do.

I believe prayer has to be a way of life. It is not just something we say before meals or a rote thing we read off a card. It is how we live our lives. It is what we are giving back to God for all the gifts He has given us.

Yes, prayer is different for everyone. Prayer varies during different seasons of our lives. Our goal would be to make our life a prayer.

Talk to God about your prayer life. What is it like? Is it a one-way conversation like mine is way too often? Ask God what you can do to make it better. Keep making yourself the best you can be. Make your life a prayer. Talk to God about how you can do it. I will pray for you.

GRACE THROUGH THE SEASONS

CHAPTER 10

Gifts for the Journey

I have to say, my most precious gift is my faith: the seed that was planted within me at my baptism and enriched by my mom, my teachers, and my music. My life has graced me in immeasurable ways.

My next gift has been my husband. We have been married for fifty-one years. All of those years have not been perfect, but we have grown so much in walking through them together. Rob chose to live his life in grace, and he chose me to be a part of it.

His service to the Lord has blessed me over and over in my life. Together we have done marriage preparation with almost one hundred couples. Do you think God has used our life challenges to grace others? He sure has over and over again. Rob has baptized many, many babies. I pass out the booklets at these baptisms, and I am moral support to the man I love. We have done funerals together and put on marriage workshops together. God pours His blessings on us for choosing love when Satan was trying very hard to convince us otherwise.

Those three children I spoke of at the beginning of this book have indeed been precious gifts from God. I have watched them grow into mature adults who love the Lord. They have gifted us with eleven awesome grandchildren, and it would take another book to describe all of their gifts. I have learned a lot from my children and grandchildren as I hope they have from me.

God has gifted me with special friends who have been there for me through so much. Their patience and compassion have graced me through many tearful encounters. Both their prayers and their silence have truly been gifts in my life.

My music has been a special gift that the Lord gave me at age twelve and continues to bless me with. He gave it to me, and I give it back to Him every weekend at church. Music has brought me much peace, much joy, and much growth.

God has also gifted me with the gift of teaching children. Oh, I have done that for so many years. I started when I was eighteen and still teach today. God's children are mine to love and teach the best way I can. What a joy it is to share that gift!

You see, God gives us all gifts to share with others. He doesn't want us to keep them for ourselves. We are a communal people. We need each other. We need to share and love one another in any way we can. What gifts has God given you to share? Have you? Can you? Will you? We can all pray for others. Prayer is such an important gift. Reflect on your life of giving. Talk to God. Thank God for what He has given you.

GRACE THROUGH THE SEASONS

CHAPTER 11

I Believe There Is More

Open your eyes and look around. There is so much to do in our world. If you are reading this book, there is still more to do. It doesn't matter if you are fifteen or ninety-five. I am always asking the Lord what is next. *What do you want of me now, Lord?* I remember when I was forty-five and He wanted me to go back to college to get a master's degree in school counseling. I told Him I was too old and too tired—no way! But in the end, I did as He asked and had sixteen beautiful years as a school counselor. He knew I wasn't too old. He knew what I needed. I just needed a push.

When I was seventy and asked to be on another Cursillo team, I said, "Oh no, Lord. I'm too tired to stay up that late." In the end I went and, due to someone's backing out, was asked to give a talk on piety. It was such a blessing in my life. God knows what is best for me. I had an eighty-six-year-old at my table who blessed me with her youthful responses and enthusiasm all weekend. God put her there to show me He wasn't and isn't through with me yet. I'm just a young seventy-year-old.

Yes, I believe there is more—more to do and more *grace* to grab onto. There are more gifts to give, more joy to share, more compassion to spread, and more prayers to be said. And of course, more love is needed in this world of ours. If we but stay open to the gentle whispers of the Holy Spirit, we will be guided to what exactly the *more* is in our lives. The song "I Believe There is More" by Don Moen says it all if you listen with your hearts.

How about you? Do you believe there is more? Do you ask God for more in your life? Do you shy away from asking that? Are you afraid of what God might ask of you? You may have heard it said that God won't give you more than you can handle. But you have to trust Him. You have to believe that He will give you all you need when He asks more of you. Go on now and ask Him, "What do you want of me, Lord?"

_____

_____

_____

_____

_____

_____

_____

_____

_____

_____

_____

_____

_____

_____

_____

_____

_____

_____

_____

_____

_____

GRACE THROUGH THE SEASONS

CHAPTER 12

Grace... What a Gift!

Grace is a gift given to us from our good and gracious God! What we do with His grace is completely up to us. We can be enriched by grace and grow in our love, or we can turn our back on grace and forget how to love. God is so good that He gives us a free will to make that choice. I just can't imagine what my life would have been like without the grace of God. He has brought me through so many things. He has taught me so much. He has blessed me abundantly.

Thank You, Lord, for Your gift of sanctifying grace at my baptism. Thank You for the gifts of sacramental grace when I received confirmation, marriage, reconciliation, and the Eucharist. Thank You especially for the Eucharist in my life. Each time I receive You, I am enriched with Your love, Your blessings, Your courage, and Your wisdom. You are truly a gift to me! Thank You for the actual graces, the interventions in my life, poured out by the Holy Spirit each and every day. Every day in prayer I say it, but now I say it publicly in this writing: Thank You, Lord, for the gift of *grace* in my life. Here are some beautiful song suggestions about grace that you can take to prayer: "Your Grace Finds Me" by Matt Redman, "Your Grace Still Amazes Me" by Steve Green, "Your Grace is Enough" by Chris Tomlin, "Call It Grace" by Unspoken, and "Grace Wins" by Matthew West.

Thank you, the reader, for taking the time to read about my life in grace. I pray it has helped you reflect on yours. I pray you choose to live each day becoming more like Jesus while living your life in *Grace Through the Seasons*. I pray your eyes and ears are awakened to the grace all around you and in you. I ask all this in the name of our Lord Jesus. Amen.

REVIEWS

Michael Casey, in his book *Balaam's Donkey*, writes, "When Jesus promises that faith the size of a mustard seed can be instrumental in uprooting mulberry bushes and casting them into the sea, he is making a point about the smallness of our efforts compared with the magnitude of divine grace…The key component is faith—our connection with God which makes the impossible thinkable and doable." That is a good summary of Joyce Heiple's book *Grace Through the Seasons*.

Here Joyce Heiple examines her life in the light of God's grace. Her spiritual autobiography challenges her readers to do the same. Her very personal style makes this book seem like a conversation between her and the reader. Her challenging reflection questions come from her background as an educator, counselor, and spiritual director.

—Msgr. Charles Beebe, PA
Diocese of Peoria, Illinois

Using her own life as a testimony to God's grace, Joyce Heiple invites us to reflect on the challenging, courageous, and contrary moments in our own lives and mind God's presence in their very midst. We discover our lives are another scripture written by God.
—Albert Haase, OFM, author of *Becoming an Ordinary Mystic: Spirituality for the Rest of Us*

HOPE! From the first chapter to the last, hope reigns through this book. Very well written, the first-person perspective shows how the God of this universe works through His grace to give us hope and that unconditional love given to every person without merit. Each chapter demonstrates the "grace-filled" moments in Joyce's life and how He did not abandon her. I would recommend this reading to anyone who is in need of God's grace and hope.
—Pastor Bob DeBolt, Washburn Christian Church

If anyone reading this book would be interested in having a talk given on Grace, please email me at: heiple5@mtco.com

ABOUT THE AUTHOR

Joyce Heiple is a woman who loves the Lord with all her being. She wrote this book *Grace Through the Seasons* in response to the Holy Spirit urging she felt within. Joyce has been an Elementary teacher and a School Counselor. She is a musician, a mother, a grandmother, a wife, a spiritual director, a speaker, and a steadfast Christian.

CPSIA information can be obtained
at www.ICGtesting.com
Printed in the USA
LVHW051611040221
678389LV00014B/2033